T0015852

How Is a Turbine Like a Whale Fin?
Machines Imitating Nature

Walt Brody

Lerner Publications • Minneapolis

Lerner Publications Company
An imprint of Lerner Publishing Group, Inc.
241 First Avenue North
Minneapolis, MN 55401 USA

For reading levels and more information, look up this title at www.lernerbooks.com.

Main body text set in Billy Infant Regular. Typeface provided by SparkType.

Editor: Brianna Kaiser **Designer:** Martha Kranes
Lerner team: Sue Marquis

Library of Congress Cataloging-in-Publication Data

Names: Brody, Walt, 1978- author.
Title: How is a turbine like a whale fin? : machines imitating nature / Walt Brody.
Description: Minneapolis, MN : Lerner Publications Company, [2022] | Series: Lightning Bolt Books Imitating Nature | Includes bibliographical references and index. | Audience: Ages 6–9. | Audience: Grades 2–3. | Summary: "People use machinery in their lives every day. But how do they make machinery more efficient? They turn to nature! Biomimicry has led to many innovative robots and machines, and readers can explore them here"— Provided by publisher.
Identifiers: LCCN 2020014636 (print) | LCCN 2020014637 (ebook) | ISBN 9781728404196 (lib. bdg.) | ISBN 9781728418438 (eb pdf)
Subjects: LCSH: Aerofoils—Juvenile literature. | Fins (Anatomy)—Juvenile literature. | Biomimicry—Juvenile literature.
Classification: LCC TL574.A4 B768 2021 (print) | LCC TL574.A4 (ebook) | DDC 629.8/92—dc23

LC record available at https://lccn.loc.gov/2020014636
LC ebook record available at https://lccn.loc.gov/2020014637

Manufactured in the United States of America
1-48477-48991-12/22/2020

Table of Contents

Inventions from Nature

Engineers design machines and robots. Machines and robots help people. They make people's lives easier.

Some ideas for machines and robots come from nature. This is called biomimicry. *Bio* means "living." *Mimic* means "to copy."

Engineers make drawings of machines and robots. These drawings are called blueprints.

A Whale's Fin

Whales are some of the largest animals. Humpback whales can be up to 60 feet (18 m) long! They weigh up to 40 tons (36 t).

Humpback whales' fins are longer than any other whale fins. Their fins have bumps on them. The bumps make water move smoothly around the fins and make humpbacks excellent swimmers.

Humpbacks' pectoral fins can grow up to 16 feet (5 m) long.

Wind turbines make energy. Engineers have designed new turbine blades with bumps on them, just as whale fins have.

The company Whalepower designed new turbine blades that mimic humpbacks' fins.

The new turbine design makes more energy than other wind turbines. Their energy is more efficient, which is good for the environment.

A Robot Cockroach

Cockroaches are small insects and pests. They can fit into tiny places. Most people do not want them crawling around their homes.

There are more than 4,000 species of cockroaches.

Cockroaches have been on Earth for more than three hundred million years. They can live without a head for a week.

Engineers at the University
of California, Berkeley,
have made a new robot.
It is small like a cockroach.
It can help find missing
people.

These little robots can fit in places where humans cannot fit. They can move quickly too. They are perfect for moving through rubble to find survivors.

The cockroach robots could potentially find survivors more quickly than humans could.

A Robot Manta Ray

Manta rays are huge fish. They can grow to be 29 feet (8.8 m) wide.

They are gentle giants of the ocean. They are also excellent swimmers. Their long fins glide through the water.

Manta rays have the biggest brains of any fish.

An engineer at the National University of Singapore made a manta ray robot. It looks like a manta ray but is only 25 inches (63 cm) wide.

Manta ray robots can be used in search and rescue missions. Or they can inspect underwater sea life. They can swim for up to ten hours.

Manta ray robots could assist search teams in rescue missions.

A Beetle's Shell

Many places around the world have little fresh water. But animals have ways to get the water they need.

Fog appears every morning in the Namib Desert in Africa. The Namib Desert beetle has a special shell. It collects water from the fog for the beetle to drink.

Water travels from the Namib Desert beetle's shell to its mouth so it can drink.

Scientists made a device that mimics the beetle's shell. The device can collect water. The water is given to people in need.

A device modeled after the Namib beetle helps turn fog into drinking water.

The Future of Robots

Engineers are finding ways to make humanoid robots. They look human and walk on two legs. They can be useful for many things. They can go places that would be dangerous for humans. This can help save lives. Humanoid robots tend to be slow, but they will improve in the future.

Glossary

biomimicry: getting ideas for inventions from nature

blade: a flat spinning part on wind turbines

engineer: a person who designs or builds machines

fog: a cloudlike area of small water droplets that is near the ground

pest: an animal that can bother or harm humans

rescue: an organized effort to find a missing or trapped person

robot: a machine that performs a programmed task

wind turbine: a machine that transforms wind into energy

Learn More

Ducksters: The Environment—Wind Energy
https://www.ducksters.com/science/environment
/wind_power.php

Golusky, Jackie. *Space Exploration Robots*.
Minneapolis: Lerner Publications, 2021.

Kiddle: Bionics Facts for Kids
https://kids.kiddle.co/Bionics

Kiddle: Robot Facts for Kids
https://kids.kiddle.co/Robot

Schaefer, Lola. *Robots on the Job*. Minneapolis:
Lerner Publications, 2021.

Swanson, Jennifer. *Beastly Bionics: Rad Robots,
Brilliant Biomimicry, and Incredible Inventions
Inspired by Nature*. Washington, DC: National
Geographic, 2020.

Index

Photo Acknowledgments

Image credits: jesterpop/Shutterstock.com, p. 4; cherezoff/Shutterstock.com, p. 5; Sean Steininger/Shutterstock.com, p. 6; Nico Faramaz/Shutterstock.com, p. 7; Tannis Toohey/Toronto Star/Getty Images, p. 8; Herlanzer/Shutterstock.com, p. 9; Mr.Pattrawut Yamyeunyong/Shutterstock.com, p. 10; Victor1153/Shutterstock.com, p. 11; © University of California at Berkeley, p. 12; nickpeps/Shutterstock.com, p. 13; Protograph/Shutterstock. com, p. 14; Lewis Burnett/Shutterstock.com, p. 15; Xinhua/Alamy Stock Photo, p. 16; charl898/Shutterstock.com, p. 17; imageBROKER.com/Shutterstock.com, p. 18; Martin Harvey/Alamy Stock Photo, p. 19; Udo Kieslich/Shutterstock.com, p. 20.

Cover images: Martin Prochazkacz/Shutterstock.com; Loyd Towe/Shutterstock.com.